PUFFIN

The Solar System

PUFFIN BOOKS

6
INTRODUCTION

10
THE SOLAR SYSTEM

18
THE SUN

22
THE ROCKY PLANETS

MERCURY	24
VENUS	30
EARTH	36
MARS	42

48
THE ASTEROID BELT

PUFFIN LITTLE

Little Scientist

PUFFIN BOOKS

UK | USA | Canada | Ireland | Australia
India | New Zealand | South Africa | China

Penguin
Random House
Australia

Penguin Random House Australia is part of the Penguin Random House group of companies whose addresses can be found at global.penguinrandomhouse.com.

First published by Puffin Books, an imprint of Penguin Random House Australia Pty Ltd, in 2020

Text copyright © Penguin Random House Australia Pty Ltd 2020
Puffin branding copyright © Penguin Books 2020

The moral right of the author has been asserted.

All rights reserved. No part of this publication may be reproduced, published, performed in public or communicated to the public in any form or by any means without prior written permission from Penguin Random House Australia Pty Ltd or its authorised licensees.

Other internal images: © Regina F. Silva/Shutterstock.com, © runLenarun/Shutterstock.com, © Helen Lane/Shutterstock.com, © AleksOrel/Shutterstock.com,
© Hulinska Yevheniia/Shutterstock.com, © Galina's Tales/Shutterstock.com

Cover design by Ngaio Parr © Penguin Random House Australia Pty Ltd
Internal design © Penguin Random House Australia Pty Ltd

Printed in China

A catalogue record for this book is available from the National Library of Australia

ISBN 978 1 76 089703 1

Penguin Random House Australia uses papers that are natural and recyclable products, made from wood grown in sustainable forests. The logging and manufacture processes are expected to conform to the environmental regulations of the country of origin.

penguin.com.au

52
THE GAS GIANTS

JUPITER   54

SATURN   60

URANUS   66

NEPTUNE   72

. . . .

78
THE DWARF PLANETS

86
BEYOND ...

. . . .

FAST FACTS **90**
GLOSSARY **92**
PUFFIN QUIZ **94**

CONTENTS

HELLO, LITTLE SCIENTISTS

WELCOME TO SPACE...

INTRODUCTION

I'm thrilled you're joining me on my super space adventure.

We're going to have so much fun exploring the SOLAR SYSTEM together!

THE SOLAR SYSTEM IS MASSIVE

It's hard to imagine just how massive the solar system is all the way from Earth, which is why we're off on an adventure to find out!

As Little Scientists there are always lots of new and exciting things to discover about space and the other worlds around us.

We might be LITTLE, but we've got some BIG facts to learn.

Are you ready?

Then turn the page …

INTRODUCTION

WHAT IS THE SOLAR SYSTEM?

THE SOLAR SYSTEM

The solar system is made up of our star – the sun – and everything that orbits around the sun, including planets, moons, asteroids and comets.

✷ ORBIT ✷

An orbit is the path that an object takes in space when it goes around a star, a planet or a moon.

Earth and all the other planets in the solar system orbit the sun.

In the time it takes Earth to orbit the sun – from the first day of Earth's orbit to its last – you will have celebrated a birthday, moved up a class at school and maybe even grown a few centimetres so you're not as **LITTLE** as you used to be!

That's because it takes a full year – **365 days** – for Earth to orbit the sun.

EARTH'S ORBIT

EARTH

SUN

THE SOLAR SYSTEM

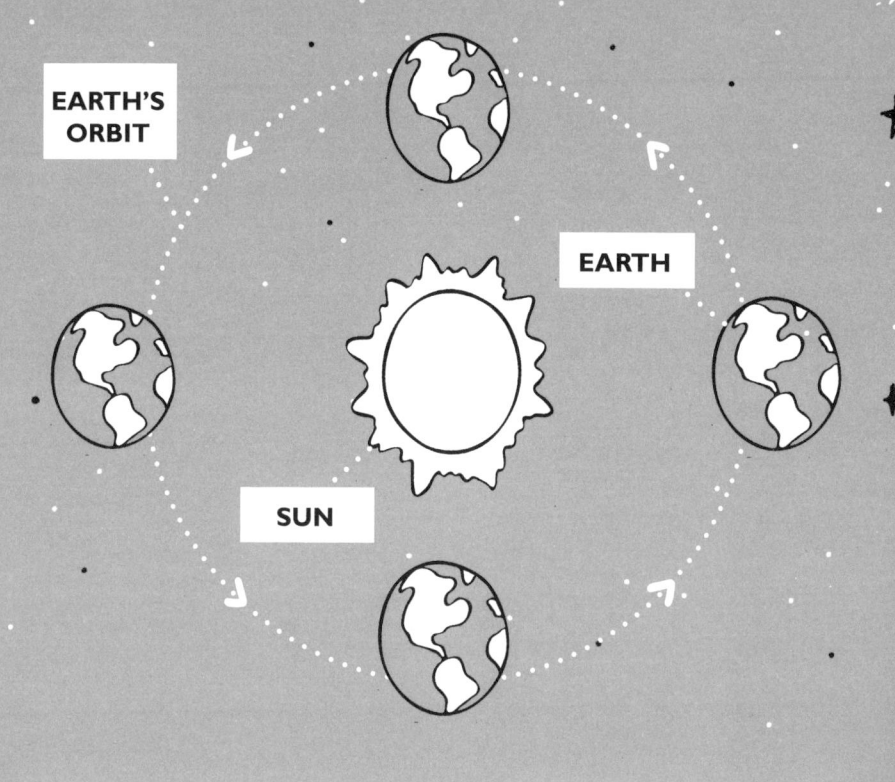

While each planet is orbiting the sun, it is also rotating on its axis. This determines the length of the planet's day. It takes a full day – 24 hours – for Earth to complete a rotation.

AXIS

13

WHAT IS A PLANET?

We now know all about how planets rotate and orbit the sun, but what is a planet?

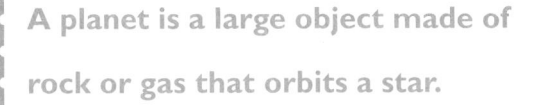

A planet is a large object made of rock or gas that orbits a star.

There are millions of large objects in the solar system orbiting our star – the sun.

So what makes planets different?

14

Big Scientists decided that for an object to be called a planet it must:

- Orbit the sun.
- Be round in shape, or nearly round.
- And it must **not** have other objects in the way of its orbit of the sun.

There are two groups of planets in the solar system, the **Rocky Planets** that are closest to the sun and the **Gas Giants** that are further away.

Let's leave the rocket ship here, jump in my planet-hopper and take a look at these planets that call the solar system their home.

THE SOLAR SYSTEM

There are **EIGHT PLANETS** in the solar system. Each planet is unique, and we're going to learn lots of fascinating facts about these other worlds when we get a little closer.

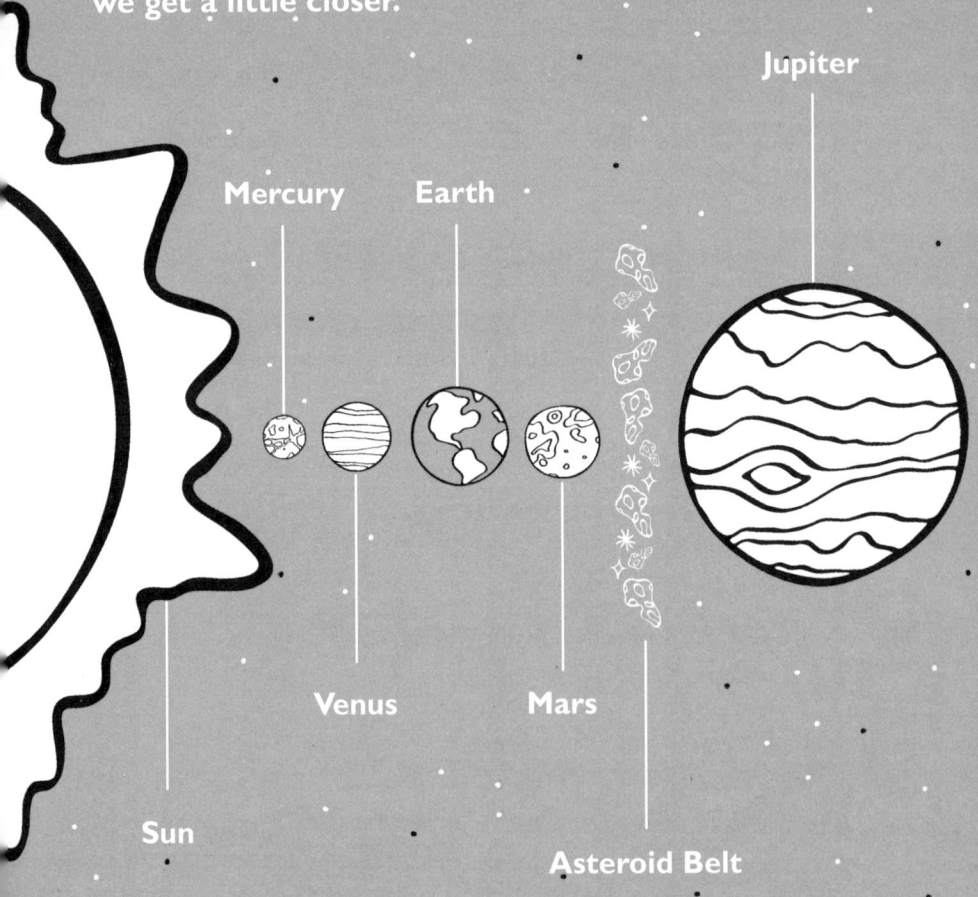

Jupiter

Mercury

Earth

Venus

Mars

Sun

Asteroid Belt

Let's get exploring!
First stop . . .
THE SUN!
Saturn
Uranus
Neptune

THE SUN

Temperature:	The average surface temp is 5700°C. Earth's average surface temp is 20°C.
Size:	The sun is the biggest object in the solar system. If it were hollow, it would take about **ONE MILLION** Earths to fill it.
Did you know?	The sun – the heart of the solar system – is a star. A star is a hot ball of glowing gases.
What's in the name?	Big Scientists call the sun a yellow dwarf star. This is the name for medium-sized stars.

FAST FACTS

Here we are, Little Scientists! We have reached the heart of the solar system. Being this close to the sun is pretty hot, so let's not stay too long!

The sun is a star, and just like the stars we see in the night sky, it is a hot ball of glowing gases. It seems different to the tiny twinkles we look at before we go to sleep, and that's because the sun is much closer to us than any other star.

From Earth, we look at the sun rising and setting every day. The sun gives us light, heat and energy, and without it, life on Earth would not exist.

It would be so cold that no living thing could survive and our planet would be completely frozen.

But the sun has one other very important job – it also plays the role of a big anchor. The sun creates **gravity** that keeps all the planets in their place. If it weren't for the sun, the planets would fly off into the universe!

✦ GRAVITY ✦

Gravity is an invisible force that pulls objects towards a planet or a star.

Earth's gravity is what keeps your feet on the ground, and the sun's gravity is what keeps all the planets in the solar system in their orbits.

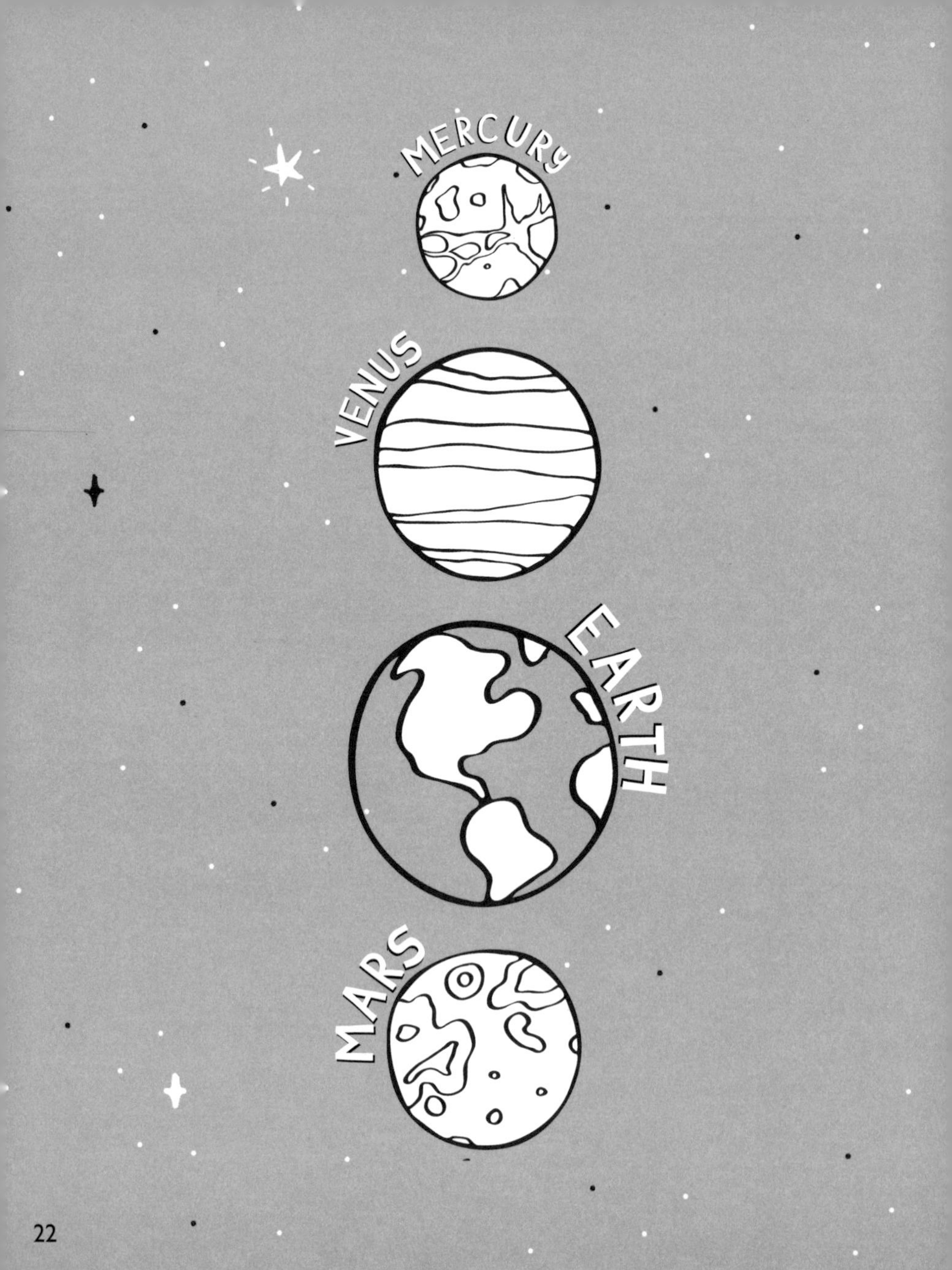
MERCURY
VENUS
EARTH
MARS

The first stop on our super space adventure is the four planets closest to the sun.

These are the **ROCKY PLANETS** – **MERCURY**, **VENUS**, **EARTH** and **MARS**.

They are called rocky planets because – yes, you guessed it – they are mostly made of rock. In fact, these planets all have a solid surface, and the core (the middle, deep inside) is mainly made of iron.

THE ROCKY PLANETS

MERCURY

Distance from the sun:	58 million kilometres
Length of day:	59 Earth days
Length of year:	88 Earth days
Did you know?	Mercury is the smallest planet in the solar system.
What's in the name?	Because of Mercury's fast orbit of the sun, the Romans named the planet after the swift-footed messenger of the gods, Mercury.

FAST FACTS

Little Scientists! We've made it to **MERCURY**, the first and smallest planet on our super space adventure!

As Mercury is so close to the sun, it has the shortest orbit of any of the planets in the solar system. It completes an orbit around the sun in just **88 days**!

Although Mercury orbits the sun quickly, it rotates on its axis very slowly. It takes Mercury **59 days** to complete a rotation!

So because Mercury has a **short year** (fast orbit) and a **long day** (slow spin), it takes a long time for the sun to rise and set there. In fact, Mercury only has one sunrise every **180 Earth days!**

Seeing as Mercury is the closest planet to the sun, it must be the **hottest** planet in the solar system, right? **WRONG!**

This is because Mercury has almost no **atmosphere**, so the heat that comes to it from the sun quickly escapes back into space.

✶ ATMOSPHERE ✶

An atmosphere is a layer of gases that surrounds a planet.

Earth's atmosphere traps heat from the sun, making the temperature on Earth comfortable for living beings. Earth's atmosphere is also made up of a mixture of gases, one of these gases is oxygen. We call this **air**, and it is essential for life.

Mercury's very thin atmosphere means it is exposed to **EXTREME** temperatures and no living thing can survive there. In the daytime it can reach highs of 430°C, but at night it can drop to minus 180°C.

I don't think we want to hop over to Mercury for a holiday any time soon – those temperatures aren't very nice at all!

Okay, Little Scientists, we've learnt about Mercury's **orbit** and **rotation**, its **boiling** and **freezing temperatures** and its **thin atmosphere**. Now we're going to check out the surface of this rocky world!

MERCURY'S CRATERS

The surface of Mercury is covered with craters. These craters formed when asteroids hit the planet.

In fact, it is filled with more craters than any other planet in the solar system. Every single crater on Mercury has a name – they are named after famous writers and artists.

MERCURY

Oh look! That's the Beethoven crater. And over there is the Shakespeare crater.

VENUS

Distance from the sun:	108 million kilometres
Length of day:	243 Earth days
Length of year:	225 Earth days
Did you know?	Venus is the hottest planet in the solar system, temperatures reach around 465°C!
What's in the name?	Named after the Roman goddess of love and beauty, Venus is the only planet to be named after a goddess and not a god.

FAST FACTS

Next up on our super space adventure is the second planet in the solar system – **VENUS**. We're going to need sunglasses to check out this spectacular planet!

Venus is the **brightest** planet in the solar system, which is why ancient astronomers named it after the Roman goddess of love and beauty.

The only objects in the sky brighter than Venus are the sun and Earth's moon.

Venus is beautiful to look at, but it might not be such a lovely place to visit . . . I hope you put your sunscreen on because Venus is the **hottest** planet in the solar system. It's not as close to the sun as Mercury, but its thick **atmosphere** traps the heat and keeps Venus toasty warm.

Although Venus has a thick atmosphere, it is not one we can breathe. It is mostly made up of **carbon dioxide (CO_2)** and the whole planet is covered with clouds of **sulphuric acid!**

Because of these acid clouds we can't see the rocky surface of Venus, so we're going to have to dive down and take a look.

Under the toxic clouds, the surface of Venus is **boiling hot**, **dry** and **rocky**.

There are no oceans because it is far too hot for water, and it is covered with deep canyons, mountains and volcanoes! In fact, Venus has more volcanoes than any other planet in the solar system.

Right, Little Scientists, let's get away from the scorching heat. We've got one more fact to find out …

Venus takes **225 Earth days** to orbit the sun and **243 Earth days** to rotate on its axis. This means that Venus's **day** is **longer** than its **year!**

Not only does Venus rotate on its axis very slowly, it also rotates **backwards!**

That's right, Little Scientists, Venus spins in the opposite direction to Earth and most of the other planets.

⭑ Retrograde Rotation ⭑

This is the description Big Scientists gave to a planet that rotates backwards on its axis.

There are only two planets in the solar system with retrograde rotation – **Venus** and **Uranus**.

EARTH

Distance from the sun:	150 million kilometres
Length of day:	24 Earth hours
Length of year:	365 Earth days
Did you know?	Earth is the only planet in the solar system (that we know of) that can support life.
What's in the name?	Earth is the only planet that wasn't named after a Greek or Roman god or goddess. The word 'Earth' is Old English meaning ground or soil.

FAST FACTS

This planet needs no introduction, the third rock from the sun and the place we all live – **PLANET EARTH!**

Our home is one of the most special planets in the solar system and here's why ...

The conditions on Earth are perfect for humans, animals and plants to survive. And, as far as Big Scientists know, it is the only planet in the solar system with living things on it.

So what makes Earth so different to all the other planets?

HOME SWEET HOME!

EARTH IS COVERED WITH WATER!

Liquid water is what allows life to exist on Earth, and more than 70 per cent of the Earth's surface is covered by oceans.

If Earth was any closer to the sun, all the water would evaporate and if it was further away, it would freeze.

Earth is what's called a **goldilocks planet**. Unlike the other planets in the solar system, it's not too hot, and not too cold – **it's just right** – like the porridge in the story of *Goldilocks and the Three Bears*.

WE CAN BREATHE THE AIR!

Earth is the only planet in the solar system with an atmosphere that can support living things.

Not only does Earth's atmosphere contain the **oxygen (O^2)** that we need to breathe, this blanket of gases also protects us from the blasting heat of the sun. It warms our planet by day and cools it at night.

Over **7 billion** people live on Earth, as well as millions of species of plants and animals. So far, Big Scientists have not found any other planet that would make a good home for us, so it is important that we take care of our precious planet.

EARTH'S MOON

A moon is an object that orbits a planet. Other planets in the solar system have lots of moons, but Earth only has one moon and it is our nearest neighbour in space.

The moon is the brightest object in the night sky. However, the moon does not shine with its own light, it reflects light coming from the sun.

Earth's moon is the only place beyond Earth where humans have set foot. On **20 July 1969**, the astronauts of America's **Apollo 11** mission landed on the moon.

EARTH

MARS

Distance from the sun:	228 million kilometres
Length of day:	24.6 Earth hours
Length of year:	687 Earth days
Did you know?	Mars has four seasons, just like Earth.
What's in the name?	Mars is often called the Red Planet, because of its reddish colour. In ancient times people associated its red colour with warfare. That is why Mars was named for the Roman god of war.

FAST FACTS

Welcome, Little Scientists, to the fourth world from the sun and the last of the rocky planets – **MARS!**

Hop on the Mars rover and let's get exploring.

Mars is often called the **Red Planet**, because of its reddish colour. Big Scientists now know that Mars is red because of large amounts of **iron oxide**, or rust, in the rocks and dust on its surface.

Even though humans haven't set foot on the surface of Mars, several missions have visited, and it is the only planet we have sent **rovers** to. These robot cars drive around Mars, taking pictures and measurements for Big Scientists to study and learn more about the Red Planet.

Mars has mountains and canyons like Earth. It is home to the solar system's biggest volcano. Big Scientists named it **Olympus Mons** and it's nearly three times larger than Mount Everest, the tallest mountain on Earth!

Mars is similar to Earth in lots of ways. A day on Mars is almost the same as a day on Earth, it's just a little bit longer. Mars even has some ice on it, but, unlike Earth, there's no liquid water anywhere on the planet because it's so cold.

So even though Mars and Earth are alike in some ways, there is a big difference.

LIVING THINGS CAN'T SURVIVE ON MARS

Mars has a very thin atmosphere which means it can't hold on to the sun's heat. This is the reason for the freezing temperatures and no liquid water. Mars's atmosphere is also mostly made of carbon dioxide, which we can't breathe.

Without oxygen and water, Mars wouldn't be a very nice place to live!

LIFE ON MARS

Because Mars is close to Earth and is so similar in some ways, people have wondered for a very long time if there was life on Mars.

In 1877 astronomers thought they saw canals on the surface of Mars in long, straight lines. They thought someone must have made them. People wrote books and stories about aliens from Mars, and they called them MARTIANS.

However, Big Scientists have never found any evidence that there has been life on Mars.

THE ASTEROID BELT

THE ASTEROID BELT

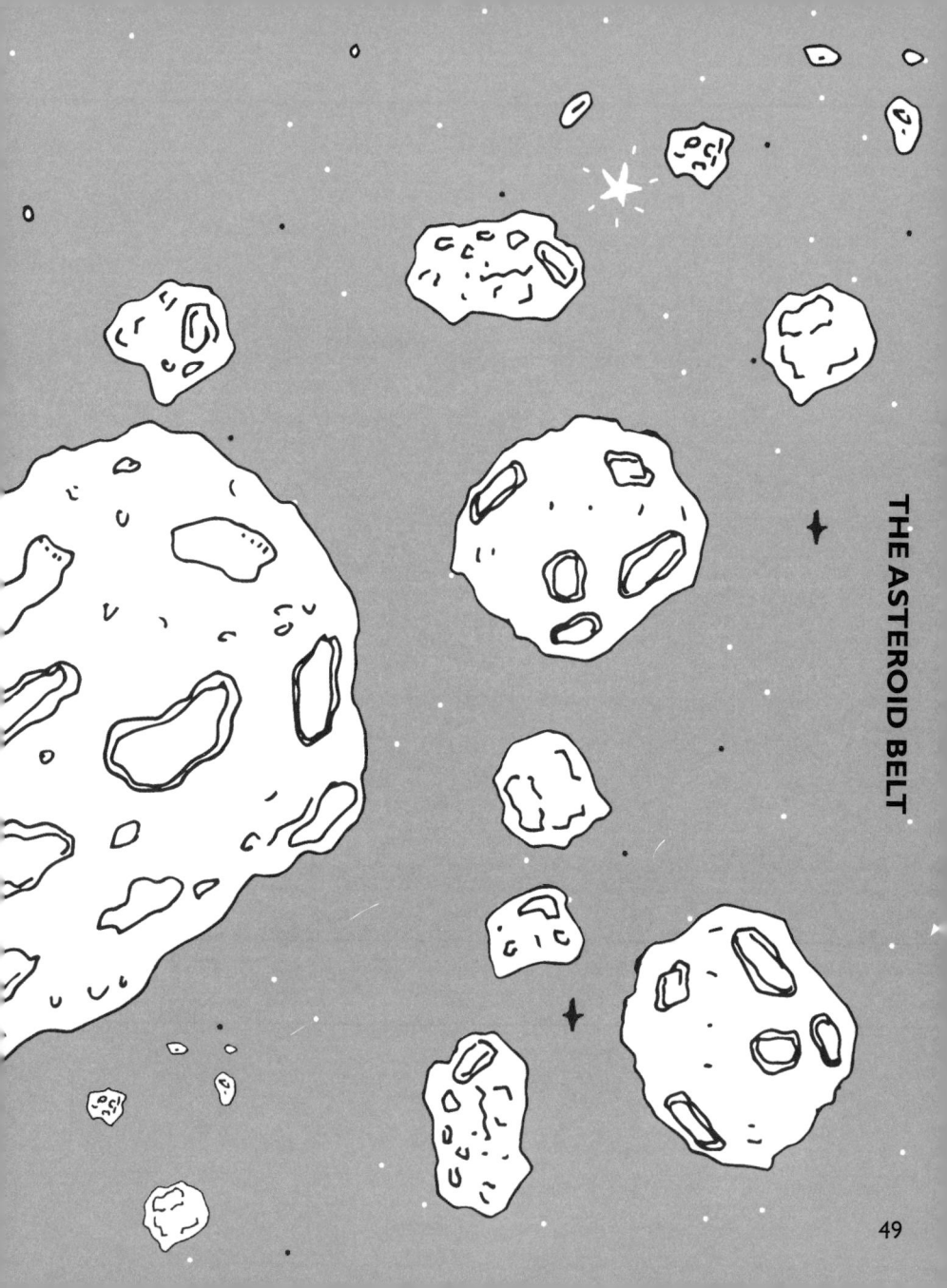

We have left Mars and the rocky planets behind us. To get to the next group of planets we need to travel through the asteroid belt.

Watch where you're going, Little Scientists, because the asteroid belt is a ring of big and little chunks of rock that orbit the sun.

Big Scientists call these rocks ASTEROIDS!

✦ WHAT IS AN ASTEROID? ✦

Asteroids are made of rock and metal. They are not planets because they have odd and irregular shapes.

Some are really big, but lots of asteroids can be as small as pebbles.

Along with many thousands of asteroids, the asteroid belt is also home to a **dwarf planet** called **Ceres**.

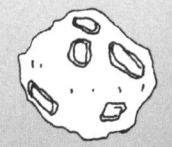

We will learn all about these dwarf planets on **page 78!**

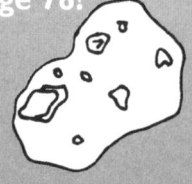

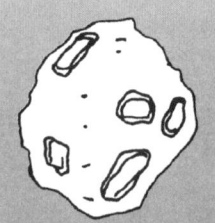

THE ASTEROID BELT

Okay, Little Scientists, we've learnt all about the sun, explored the **ROCKY PLANETS** and crossed the asteroid belt, but there is still lots more to discover.

It's time to check out the **GAS GIANTS** of the solar system – **JUPITER**, **SATURN**, **URANUS** and **NEPTUNE**.

These planets are very different from the rocky worlds we've just visited. They are much **bigger** and are made of **gas**.

Remember, we can't land on the surface of these planets because they're not solid!

THE GAS GIANTS

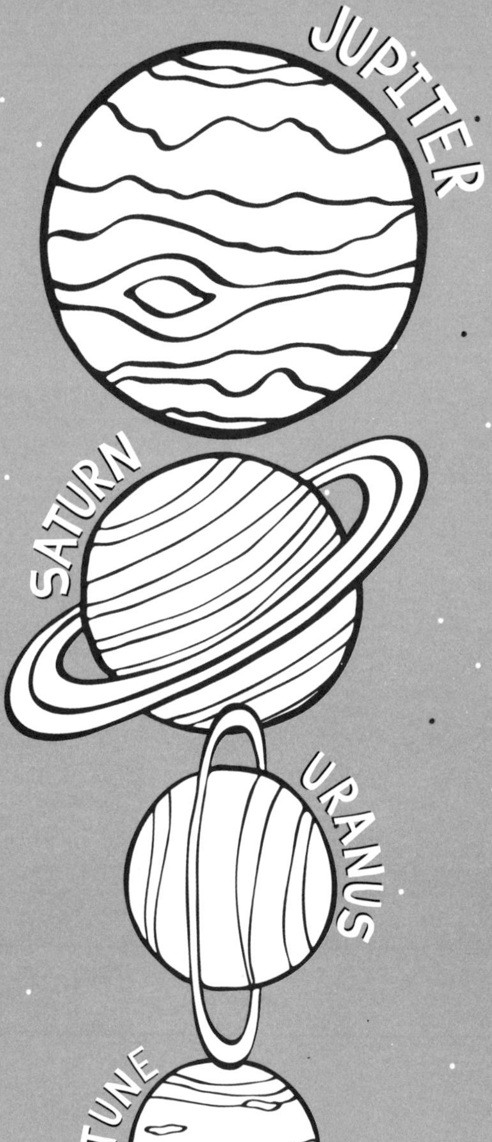

JUPITER

Distance from the sun:	778 million kilometres
Length of day:	10 Earth hours
Length of year:	11.8 Earth years
Did you know?	Jupiter is the largest planet in the solar system.
What's in the name?	Because of its size, Jupiter was named after the Roman king of the gods.

FAST FACTS

Jupiter is the BIGGEST planet in the solar system!

Here we are, Little Scientists! We have made it to the fifth planet from the sun and the first **gas giant** of our super space adventure – **JUPITER**.

Jupiter is so far from the sun that it takes more than **11 Earth years** for it to travel around once. Although Jupiter's orbit is much longer than the Earth's, its day is much shorter. Jupiter rotates once about every **10 hours**. That's faster than any other planet!

Jupiter is made of many of the same materials as stars: if it had been bigger than it is, it might have become a star!

Because Jupiter is a massive ball of swirling gases and liquids, it doesn't have a true surface. It is surrounded by thick clouds and below these clouds are thousands of kilometres of layers of hydrogen and **helium gas**.

Big Scientists don't actually know if Jupiter has a solid core because the extreme temperatures of the gas clouds would destroy any equipment sent to find out.

JUPITER

> The **BIG, RED SPOT** is bigger than Earth!

So we can't land on Jupiter because it is made of gas and there is no ground to land on …

Even if there was somewhere to land, it's no place for Little Scientists. Jupiter is a very stormy planet with wild winds whipping over the place all the time. We can even see one of its storms from Earth. Big Scientists call it the **BIG, RED SPOT** – it's the biggest hurricane in the solar system and it has been raging for hundreds of years!

JUPITER'S MOONS

There are about 79 moons orbiting the planet Jupiter!

Most of these moons are very small – only a few kilometres wide.

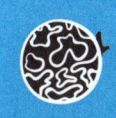

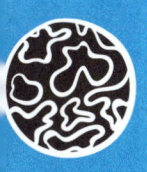

But it is the planet's four largest moons that have interested Big Scientists the most. **IO**, **EUROPA**, **GANYMEDE** and **CALLISTO** are large enough to be seen from Earth with a telescope.

GANYMEDE is the largest moon in the solar system, and is even bigger than the planet Mercury!

SATURN

Distance from the sun:	1.4 billion kilometres
Length of day:	10.7 Earth hours
Length of year:	29 Earth years
Did you know?	Saturn is the furthest planet that can be seen from Earth without a telescope.
What's in the name?	In Roman mythology, Saturn is the father of Jupiter, king of the gods. This is where Saturn got its name as it is similar to the planet Jupiter in many ways.

FAST FACTS

Up next, Little Scientists, is **gas giant** number two – **SATURN!**

Just like Jupiter, Saturn is a massive ball of gas with an atmosphere made up of **hydrogen** and **helium**. It also does not have a solid surface, but Big Scientists do think it might have a solid core deep inside.

Saturn is most famous for its beautiful rings. Did you know that all the gas giants have rings, but Saturn's rings are the most magnificent; they are bright, wide and colourful.

Come on, Little Scientists, let's take a closer look!

It seems like one big ring but there are surrounding the planet. Although they look solid from a distance, the rings are actually made of many, many pieces of ice and rock. Some are as small as a grain of sand, others are as big as a bus!

SATURN

Saturn is the second largest planet in the solar system. Even though Saturn is really big it is also very light.

Some Big Scientists think that because the gases it's made of are so lightweight, the whole planet would actually be able to float in water!

SATURN'S MOONS

In addition to Saturn's beautiful rings, many moons orbit the planet.

Saturn has 53 moons. Big Scientists have found more, but are waiting to confirm that they are actually moons. If all these moons get confirmed, Saturn will have 82 moons!

The largest of Saturn's moons is called Titan and it has its own atmosphere, which is very unusual for a moon.

SATURN

URANUS

Distance from the sun:	2.9 billion kilometres
Length of day:	17 Earth hours
Length of year:	84 Earth years
Did you know?	Uranus is the only planet that spins on its side.
What's in the name?	Uranus was named after the Greek god of the sky. According to myth, he was the father of Saturn and the grandfather of Jupiter.

FAST FACTS

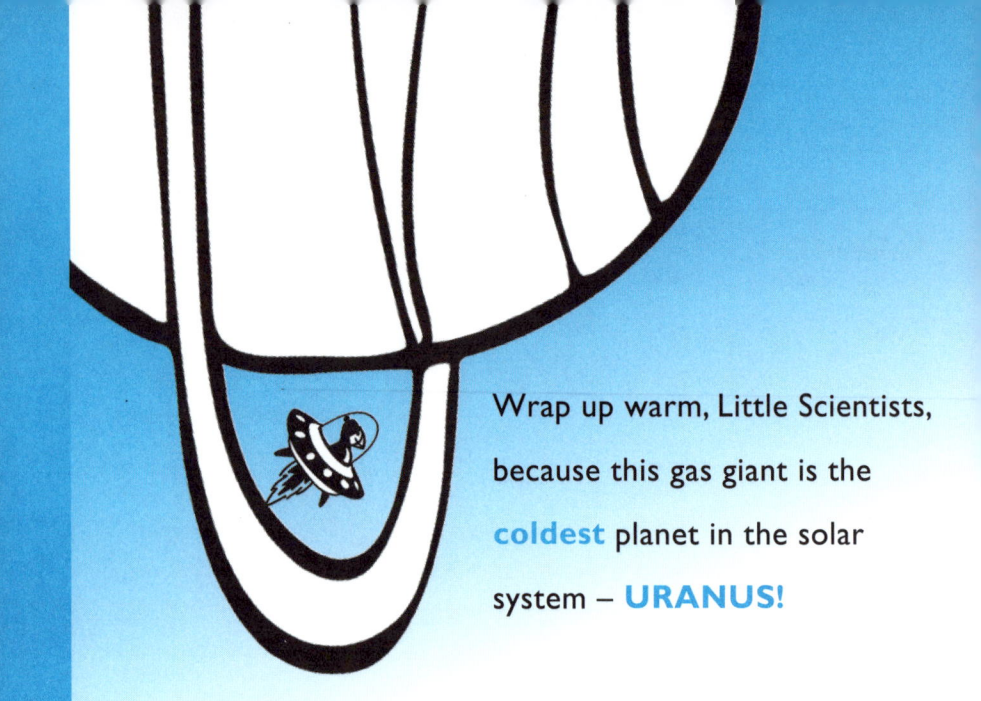

Wrap up warm, Little Scientists, because this gas giant is the **coldest** planet in the solar system – **URANUS!**

Uranus is a **gas giant**, but Big Scientists also call it an **Ice Giant** because it is made of **gas** and **icy materials**, above a small rocky centre.

Like Jupiter and Saturn, its atmosphere is a mixture of **hydrogen** and **helium**, but it also contains **methane**. It is the methane gas that gives Uranus its pretty blue-green colour.

Uranus moves very slowly around the sun. It takes the planet **84 Earth years** to complete an orbit! But it only takes **17 hours** for the planet to rotate on its axis. So Uranus has a **very long year** and a **very short day**.

Uranus is one of only two planets in the solar system to **rotate backwards** — Venus is the other. (Do you remember what this is called, Little Scientists? Check out **page 35**.)

Unlike any other planet in the solar system, Uranus is tilted so much that it actually spins sideways!

Big Scientists aren't sure why, but they think that some huge objects crashed into it a long time ago.

Just like all the other gas giants, Uranus has rings around it, but they are much smaller than Saturn's. The inner rings are narrow and dark grey. The outer rings are brightly coloured and easier to see.

Uranus also has **27 known moons** orbiting it. They are named after characters from stories by William Shakespeare and Alexander Pope.

Here are some of Uranus's moons . . .

PUCK

MIRANDA

ARIEL

OBERON

DID YOU KNOW...

A telescope is needed to see Uranus.

This means that ancient astronomers did not know Uranus existed as they didn't have the right equipment to see it.

Uranus was finally discovered in 1781 by astronomer William Herschel, and it was the first planet found with the aid of a telescope. Herschel originally thought it was a comet or a star, and it wasn't until two years later that Uranus was officially called a planet.

NEPTUNE

Distance from the sun:	4.5 billion kilometres
Length of day:	16 Earth hours
Length of year:	165 Earth years
Did you know?	Neptune is the windiest planet in the solar system.
What's in the name?	In Roman mythology Neptune was the god of the sea. The planet was named after the sea god because of its deep blue colour.

FAST FACTS

We are now **4.5 billion kilometres** from the sun, and we have finally reached the eighth and most distant planet in the solar system – **NEPTUNE!**

Because Neptune is so far out in space, it takes a very, very long time to go around the sun. Just like Uranus, Neptune has a **long year** and a **short day**. It takes the planet **165 Earth years** to complete a full orbit! But it only takes **16 hours** to rotate once on its axis.

Neptune is made mostly of hydrogen and helium, with icy materials and methane. The methane gives Neptune the same blue colour as Uranus. Because of this, Big Scientists also call this gas giant an Ice Giant.

WHY DOES METHANE MAKE A PLANET BLUE?

Planets have the colours that they have because of what they are made of and how their atmospheres reflect and absorb the light from the sun.

The atmospheres of Uranus and Neptune are made up of a lot of methane. The methane gas absorbs red light from the sun and reflects it out blue. This gives Uranus a blue-green colour, and Neptune a blue colour.

Just like his gas giant brothers, Neptune is surrounded by rings. They are not as spectacular as Saturn's rings, in fact they are very hard to see! But there are **six faint rings** surrounding the planet.

Neptune also has **13 moons** that we know about and they are all named after Greek sea gods.

TRITON

Neptune's biggest moon is called TRITON.

THE GREAT DARK SPOT

Do you remember Jupiter's big, red spot — the hurricane that has been raging for hundreds of years? Well, Neptune has the strongest winds of any planet in the solar system, and also has giant storms swirling on it. Big Scientists called one of these storms the GREAT DARK SPOT because it looked like a big blotch of dark blue.

This storm didn't last as long as the one on Jupiter. The last time astronomers pointed their telescopes at the great dark spot to take a picture of it, it had disappeared! But now a new storm has formed on another part of the planet.

THE DWARF PLANETS

THE DWARF PLANETS

We have visited all the planets in the solar system. But our super space adventure isn't over just yet. We still have a few more worlds to explore. Follow me, Little Scientists, we're off to see the **DWARF PLANETS!**

WHAT IS A DWARF PLANET?

A dwarf planet is a lot like the other eight planets in the solar system.

- They are round in shape.
- They orbit the sun.

But a dwarf planet can have a bit of a bumpy journey around the sun. Its orbit is full of other objects like asteroids. And remember, Little Scientists, to be called a planet its orbit must be clear of any other objects.

So far, Big Scientists have found five dwarf planets – PLUTO, ERIS, MAKEMAKE, HAUMEA and CERES.

Come on, Little Scientists. Let's get exploring!

Distance from the sun: 413 million kilometres
Length of day: 9 Earth hours
Length of year: 4.6 Earth years

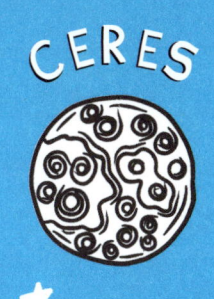

CERES

The first dwarf planet I'm going to tell you about can be found in the **asteroid belt** between Mars and Jupiter.

CERES [pronounced **SEAR-ees**] is the largest object in the asteroid belt and is the only dwarf planet in the inner solar system.

When Big Scientists first spotted it in 1801 they thought it was just another asteroid. It wasn't until 2006 that Big Scientists realised Ceres was very different to the thousands of rocks that surrounded it, and decided to call it a dwarf planet.

THE DWARF PLANETS

PLUTO

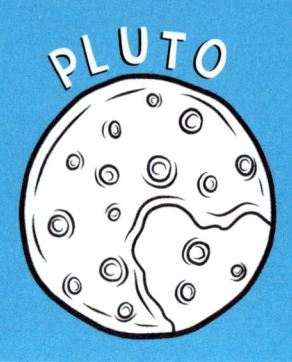

Distance from the sun: 5.9 billion kilometres
Length of day: 153 Earth hours
Length of year: 248 Earth years

Out past Neptune in the **KUIPER BELT**, an area full of icy objects and other dwarf planets, is **PLUTO**.

When Big Scientists discovered Pluto in 1930, it was named the ninth planet of the solar system. It wasn't until many years later, in 2006, that Big Scientists discovered lots of other objects in the Kuiper Belt that appeared even bigger than Pluto.

Because Pluto shares its orbit with other icy objects in the Kuiper Belt it is not a planet. So it was decided that Pluto should be called a dwarf planet.

Distance from the sun: 6.4 billion kilometres

Length of day: 4 Earth hours

Length of year: 285 Earth years

HAUMEA

Next up is **HAUMEA** [pronounced **HAW-mea**].

Big Scientists didn't discover this icy rock until very recently, in 2004.

You may have noticed its odd shape. This is because Haumea is one of the fastest rotating large objects in the solar system, which makes this dwarf planet look like a squashed ball!

THE DWARF PLANETS

MAKEMAKE

Distance from the sun: 6.8 billion kilometres

Length of day: 22 Earth hours

Length of year: 305 Earth years

Not too far from Haumea in the Kuiper Belt is **MAKEMAKE** [pronounced **MAH-kee-MAH-kee**].

Big Scientists discovered MakeMake in 2005. It is the second brightest object in the Kuiper Belt with Pluto being the brightest.

Like all the other objects in the Kuiper Belt, MakeMake is extremely cold, so living things would not be able to survive here or on any of the dwarf planets.

Distance from the sun: 10 billion kilometres

Length of day: 26 Earth hours

Length of year: 557 Earth years

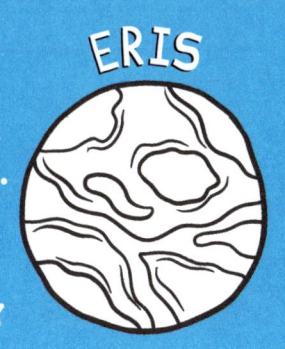

ERIS

We have finally reached the last dwarf planet – **ERIS** [pronounced **AIR-iss**]. Eris can be found billions and billions of kilometres away from the sun and is one of the largest known dwarf planets in the solar system. When it was first discovered in 2003, Big Scientists thought it might be bigger than Pluto. It was this discovery that led Big Scientists to believe that Pluto might not be a planet.

Big Scientists still have lots and lots to learn about these dwarf planets, and with each year that goes by more and more discoveries are made.

THE DWARF PLANETS

BEYOND...

BEYOND ....

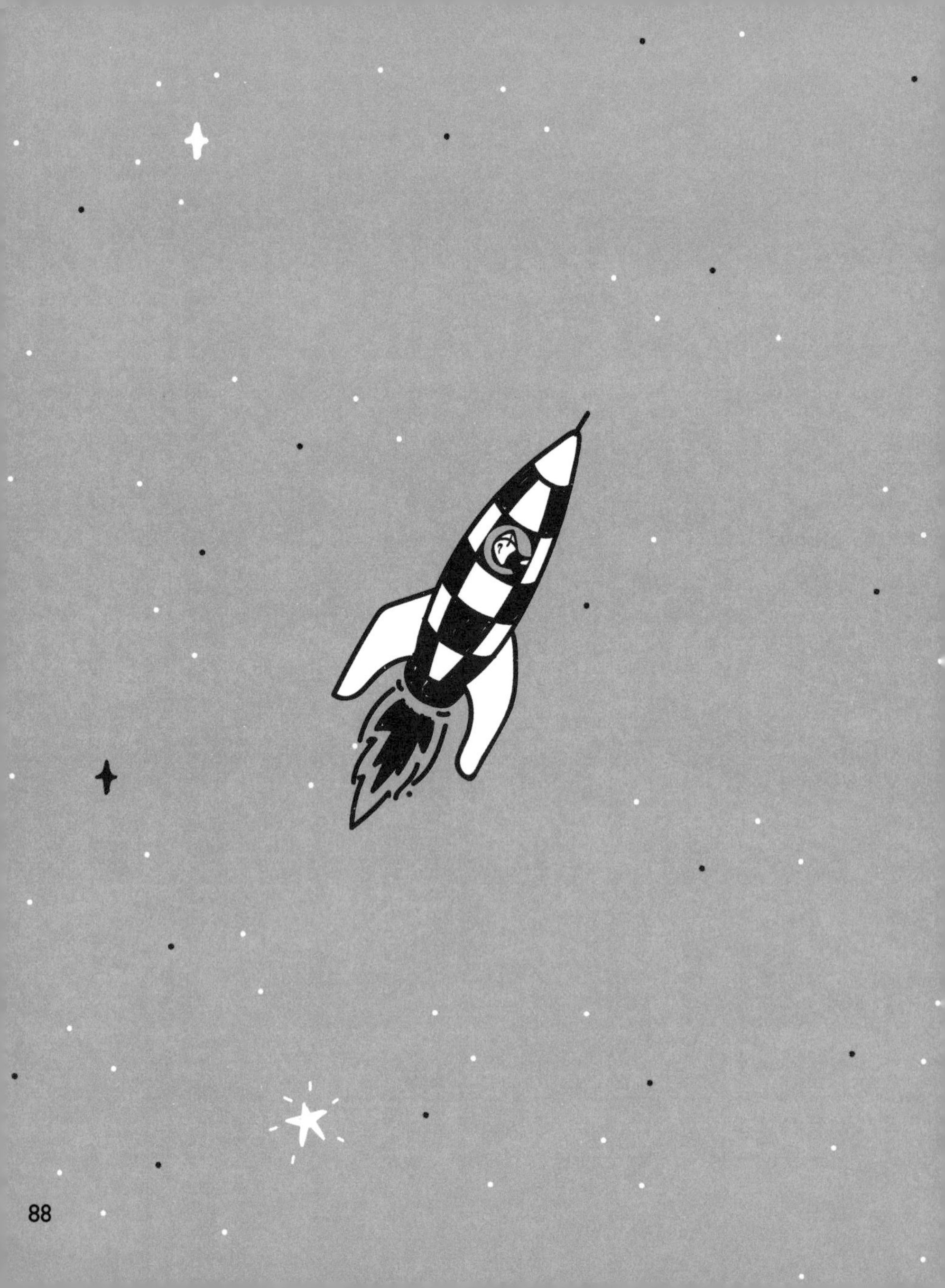

Our solar system is not the only solar system in the universe.

Big Scientists now know that lots of other stars have solar systems, just like our sun.

These other worlds are too far away for Big Scientists and spacecraft to visit. It's up to Little Scientists, like us, to keep learning **BIG** facts about the universe, and maybe, one day, we'll find a way to make it to **OUTER SPACE!**

BEYOND ...

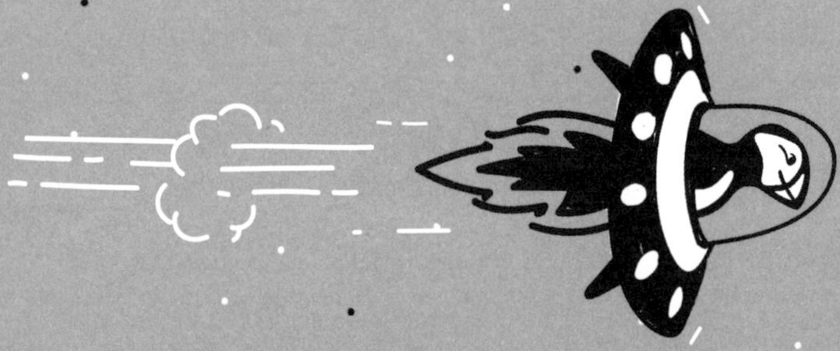

PLANET	DISTANCE FROM SUN (km)	LENGTH OF DAY Earth hrs/days	LENGTH OF YEAR Earth days/years
Mercury	58 million	59 days	88 days
Venus	108 million	243 days	225 days
Earth	150 million	24 hours	365 days
Mars	228 million	24.6 hours	687 days
Jupiter	778 million	10 hours	11.8 years
Saturn	1.4 billion	10.7 hours	29 years
Uranus	2.9 billion	17 hours	84 years
Neptune	4.5 billion	16 hours	165 years
Ceres	413 million	9 hours	4.6 years
Pluto	5.9 billion	153 hours	248 years
Haumea	6.4 billion	4 hours	285 years
MakeMake	6.8 billion	22 hours	305 years
Eris	10 billion	26 hours	557 years

FAST FACTS

GLOSSARY

ASTEROID: rock and metal with an irregular shape.

ASTEROID BELT: a ring of big and little rocks that orbit the sun.

ATMOSPHERE: a layer of gases that surrounds a planet.

AXIS: the line about which a planet turns.

DWARF PLANET: a round planet that orbits the sun but has not cleared its orbital path of other debris.

GAS GIANT: a large planet primarily made of gas.

GRAVITY: an invisible force that pulls objects towards a planet or a star.

KUIPER BELT: an area full of icy objects and dwarf planets, beyond Neptune.

MOON: an object that orbits a planet.

ORBIT: the curved path an object takes in space around a star, planet or moon.

PLANET: a large object made of rock or gas with sufficient gravity to achieve a rounded shape and to clear its orbital path.

RETROGRADE ROTATION: description of a planet that rotates backwards on its axis.

ROCKY PLANET: a planet that is mostly made of rock, with a solid surface.

SOLAR SYSTEM: the solar system consists of the sun and everything that orbits around it.

STAR: a hot ball of glowing gases.

UNIVERSE: all of space, and all the matter and energy that it contains.

GLOSSARY

PUFFIN QUIZ

1. Which planet is the fastest orbiting planet?

2. Which planet is covered largely by water?

3. Which planet is known for the **BIG, RED SPOT**?

4. Which planet is the first of the **GAS GIANTS**?

5. What sort of planet is Pluto?

ANSWERS: 1. Mercury 2. Earth 3. Jupiter 4. Jupiter 5. dwarf planet.

PUFFIN QUIZ

A PUFFIN LITTLE BOOK